Liberated Publishing

Presents...

Book of Poetry

By: Nneka J. Howell

Liberated Publishing Inc.

2519 Atwood Dr

Clarksville, TN 37040

© 2009 Nneka J. Howell

Published by: Liberated Publishing Inc

All rights reserved. No part of this book may be reproduced in any form or by any means without the prior written consent of the Publisher, excepting brief quotes used in reviews.

If you purchased this book without a cover you should be aware that this book is stolen property. It was reported as "unsold and destroyed" to the Publisher and neither the Author nor the Publisher has received any payment for this "stripped book."

ISBN **0982552319**
EAN-13 **978-0-9825523-1-5**

First Printing: March 2006

Printed in the United States of America

To whom it may concern:

These here words are not just combined syllables. They are words from the soul that serve as truth and inspiration. It is a future vision to some and a reflection for many. It is strength to others, and perhaps a weakness for plenty.

Look behind the words, and catch the true meaning.

Special Thanks to:

God

Sandra & Malcolm Banks (My parents)

Willie Mae Davis (Grandmother – R.I.P)

& Many More

Contents

Chapter 1: Friendship

- Friendship
- Build Me Up
- Paradise
- Carpet Stains
- Tambourine
- Dear Best Friend
- Would You
- Don't Fail Me Now
- I Thought Wrong
- Versus Me & You
- Never Met Me

Chapter 2: Skin Deep

- God Iz
- She Cried Herself
- The Boy
- Poetry
- Her vs. Me
- After Math
- Drowning
- Elevation Deflation
- I Stand
- Grandma
- Damaged
- To Speak

Contents

- *Real*
- *Trading Places*
- *You're A Liar*
- *Self-Contradiction*
- **Suspect**
- *Daddy*
- *Don't Let Go*
- *I Am Me*
- *Beautiful Black Woman*
- *Theme for English 3*
- *Like A Racecar*
- *Try*
- *Voice Yourself*
- *Sometimes*
- *Slaves No More*
- *The Title*
- *Conquer*
- *Testing Me*
- *No Meaning*
- *Suicide*

Chapter 3: Love, Lust, & Beyond

- *Tasty*
- *Who Do You Tell*
- *Will We Ever*
- *Love*
- *Zoom In*
- *Sweet Temptation*
- *Heart Broken*

Contents

- Dope Girl
- Heartless
- Without You
- Anonymous
- Insecure
- I want It
- Why
- Pressure
- Blind
- Love & Loyalty
- The Greatest Man

CHAPTER 1: Friendship

"Without loyalty there is nothing."

Friendship

Traces of heavy bleeding, friendship is so deceiving.

Why be the only one giving, and I want a little receiving?

Headaches from all the thinking, I've wasted some time speaking

the truth had started leaking.

Why be a savior for those who have come so incorrect?

Ask me for some help, and I say "reject."

I show no flesh, for I am self respected

any pain upon me is self inflicted.

Respect my wishes, throw away my kisses-

I have been too loyal, so forget this friendship.

There is nothing like betrayal, and nothing like loyalty-

meaning if I'm the victim, who could the suspect be?

The suspect is me, for I have not trusted thy conscience-

not so often I ignore it, and that is just nonsense.

I've lied to myself just to patch things up,

when deep inside I knew I had no choice but to give up.

Not give on me, but-

give on him, give on them, give on she.

For thy have tried to take me for granted, loyalty is sometimes limited.

For when you've tried so much, and your sick of trying-

Disloyalty can do damage until you feel like dying.

Though that is not my case, I take my pencil and erase.

Build Me Up

To whom it may concern,

I have one concern.

When I am down,

build me up.

Build me up

when I look to the sky

and I receive no answer

from the heavens above.

Build me up

brick after brick,

not stick after stick-

any rock could break that.

Build me up

when I'm lost and searching.

When my heart is hurting,

And the demons are lurking.

Build me up
because I'd build for you.
I'd build an extra layer
to show my love is true.

Build me up
when they try to break me,
and they try to make me
something that I can't be.

No, I do not expect
everybody to help build me up.
But a true friend
couldn't build enough.

When times are ruff
please build me up,
before I'm stuck like quick sand
and I just blow up.

Please build me up
when I can't hold on,
and feel like giving up-
please build me up.

I'd owe you my life
if I had six lives.
I'd give it to you twice,
by that I mean my life.

Build me up
even when I am hard on you.
The truth is
I never meant to.

Build me up
for I am not perfect.
I've made my mistakes,
and a second chance is worth it.

Build me up

I can only ask.

It's not good to beg-

as I tell the voices in my head.

Build me up

and help keep me positive.

Help support me daily

so that I can live.

Build me up

because I've been let down.

I've been lied to

and I've hit hard ground.

Build me up

because I trust in you,

and if you trust in me

You'd let me build you up too.

Build me up-

please build me up.

A true friend

couldn't build too much.

Paradise

A place that I can
escape from all pain.
Where I can't cry anymore,
and evaporate the rain.

Where the doves
are my best friend,
and dreams come true
so I don't pretend.

A place of peace
with no war with the beast.
A beautiful deep sleep
where I can be me.

Where my heart doesn't ache
and my soul doesn't cry.
I wish I knew how
to find paradise.

A place where friends
are always true.
Where every word is real
and no lie will bleed through.
Somewhere to escape to
because earth is hell.
The people I trusted most
didn't treat me well.

Sometimes life is ill
like it is dying of cancer.
Paradise please save me,
I'm on a death row.

I'm highly positive
but sometimes I feel low.
My heart pumps red blood
but I feel white like snow.

How will I know

if paradise is true?

Paradise is a place

or it might just be you.

Carpet Stains

Those friends that you knew

for a number of years

turned on you quick

and left you in tears.

CARPET STAINS

You regret something bad

that you did in the past.

Tried to forget it all,

but most memories last.

CARPET STAINS

Times are changing

and now you're a little older.

Peer pressure defeated you-

so you can't keep your head on your shoulders.

CARPET STAINS

A memory that left you scarred.

A stain on your carpet

is a stain on your heart.

It makes life hard.

THOSE CARPET STAINS

So what happens

when you try to remove the carpet?

You blame yourself

as a moving target.

CARPET STAINS

Toss them in flames

then put the fire out

and start new again.

Then again-

Those carpet stains are you.

You've blamed the world

when the whole time it was you.

When you've stained your own carpet,

what do you do?

Tambourine

Heavy breathing as if I'm an animal.

Looking through every tear drop-

I see you clear as day.

Even when it's dark out

I know what you want to say.

You keep yourself pinned

behind concrete walls.

You hide your emotions-

still, like a brick wall.

Furious

Curious

Nervous

Fearful

Put your face up to the pillow

because you thought living was too sinful.

Then you took a second guess

and thought of another way out.

You popped the top off

and poured the pills in your mouth.

Said it was painless-

the easy way out.

But I say, next time open your mouth.

I'm your friend-

I want to see the trough come out.

Now I'm stuck with a memory

of my used to be best buddy.

Now it's all pretend to me.

I guess I'll just move on-

I hope you remember me.

I'm trying to stay strong

but the devil is tempting me.

I'll be fine-

I'll ignore him, and pick up my tambourine.

Dear Best friend

I wish I had an easier way to tell you-

so I'll say it simply, I'll never fail you.

We have accomplished so much

in the little time we've known each other.

As my pen touches this paper

my heart slowly leaks.

My mind is too busy thinking-

that's why I let my pen speak.

It's like we have so much in common,

like the sister I never had.

I was wondering why God gave me three brothers,

but now I really understand.

Compared to all my friends in the past

this relationship is the most realistic.

If the world rated us for loyalty

we would be the top statistic.

You've had my back through better and worse-
and if I ever lost you I'd be hurt.
You're my footprint in the dirt-
indicating for me to walk away from the worse.

Someone I can count on
and someone I look up to.
If I ever have a problem
I know I can call on you.

Words combined can't express
how much I care for you.
I wouldn't trade you for anything-
even if the world paid me to.

My guardian angel-
something like the beautiful rainbow.
It's like you watch over me
and my life is under your halo.

We are superstars in the eyes of each other-
sisters forever from a different mother.
I don't say it that often
so I must tell you that I love you.

Even when it's difficult to get things off my chest-
I know that you're the one to help me relieve stress.
The best and nothing less-
thanks for your quality love and uniqueness.

You're the flesh and I'm the bone-
the pillow that I sleep on.
Life has been so fulfilling
and you're one of the reasons.

If I don't say it enough
I hope your reading this now.
Thanks for being honest
and thanks for being real.

Would You

Would you like me better

if I had green eyes?

A part of the crowd-

walking around with a phony smile?

What if I was rich-

never a scrape nor stitch.

Life on a platter-

easy going up the ladder.

Would you like me better

with perfect teeth?

Long hair to my back

and a voice non-weak?

What if I was poor-

would you love me then?

Would you look me in the eye

and still call me your friend?

Would you ever risk yourself
just for me?
Or does it just sound good-
you pretend to be.

Would you like me better
if I was from New York?
What if I was Muslim
and didn't eat pork?

Would you even care
if I lost a leg?
Or look at me in shame
and turn your head?

What if I was a genius-
would you envy me?
What if I was life-
would you cherish me?

Would you love me
flaws and all?
Or would you pick my leaves
until my branches fall?

Would you like me better
if I always wore a dress?
I'm not the girly type-
so would you show disrespect?

Would you ever
think deeper than deep?
Climb every mountain
until meanings greet?

Would you ever
take the best of me
and realize
I can only be me?

I am not just what you see-
I am the skin deep.
The bigger person-
I let my head speak.

I am not like the rest
but do not panic.
I live my own life
and it is not for granted.

Would you like me better
if I was someone new?
Would you love me if
I was just like you?

Don't Fail Me Now

Don't fail me now-

I've cried tears strong enough to create a fountain.

I've managed to keep my heart in place

even when climbing the biggest mountains.

Don't fail me now

because I've never failed you.

I've seen the pieces to the puzzle-

I put it together alone, for you.

Don't fail me now

because you're not the only one struggling.

Choked up by the smoke-

seems as if your smothering.

Don't fail me now

because we can make it through.

We are a team-

a bond that's irreplaceable.

Don't fail me now-
that's what they expect of you.
You're not a failure,
So you must do what's best for you.

So if that means failing me-
what are you teaching yourself?
How to run from the problem-
cause in your heart it will melt.

Don't fail me now,
I am your arm and you're my leg.
So it's safe to say without you
I'd probably lose my head.

Don't fail me now
because you'd be wasting time.
Playing games with my mind
like sparkling wine.

Don't fail me now,

I know that we can make it.

Grab a hold of my hand-

never let it go, embrace it.

Through all of these difficult phases

look at all the smiling faces.

Time races, so give it a try.

We are a team-

Just you and I.

Fail me now and my life goes by.

I Thought Wrong

Shaking your hand

was one gesture.

A tight hug

was another.

But I really meant it

that day I called you

my sister

or brother.

Even though my mother did not

birth you-

there was no limit to how much

I'd do for you.

You were never greedy-

you were once heaven sent.

Atleast I believed that

at first.

So many obstacles-

and so many dead ends.

Yet in the end I still had that ONE

good friend.

If you were my girl-

it felt good to know

I had you

in my corner.

If you were my guy-

it felt good to know

you wasn't trying to

bone.

That you

was ready to beat ass

when fellow exes did me

wrong.

But lately I've been singing

that same sad song.

The one that just repeats

OVER AND OVER.

Just when I thought I had me a

four leaf clover.

I see I was only left with

A JOKER!

So I laughed at myself

knowing that wasn't shit funny.

I felt like a slot machine.

Straight ran for my money.

All along I was thinking

maybe the problem is me.

Until I opened up my eyes-

and set my mind free.

From my knees-

I was weak.

See I was way too loyal-

so I turned the other cheek.

You dummy!

wasted too much time.

Played myself like a record-

Because time? They didn't cherish mine.

So the next time they

want to hang.

I will have a conversation with my heart-

and decide it's time for change.

I thought I had a sister-

like I thought I had a brother.

I thought I could trust you-

but I wasn't too clever.

There is no excuse-

Truth is

I didn't know the real

you.

So the only thing that I can do

is forgive.

But I'll never forget these

deceitful years.

And no

I'm not wasting time shedding tears.

One lost

is another's gain.

Throughout life

I've learned-

watch who you call your

friends.

Simply put- I THOUGHT WRONG

Versus Me & You

I'm making a stand
and you should too.
It can be the world
versus me and you.

Take the gun out of the hand
of the man with no plan.
Put brakes on the man
who robbed the store then ran.

Put hope into the child
who is scared to smile.
Tell that person who wants to give up
to run that extra mile.

Rebuild the faith in the mother
who's rape victim is her daughter.
Retrieve the ocean for the families
who are living without water.

Put the father
back into that broken home.
Give care and attention
to the children with the weakened bones.

Innocent prisoners in jail-
take them home.
Slow down the little girls
who rush to become grown.

That abandoned child-
place her in a loving home.
That stressed out graduate-
I'm wishing all of your problems gone.

I'm making a stand

and you should too.

It can be the world

versus me and you.

Replace the drugs with a book

of that dropout student.

Replace the bullets with rain

of that drive-by shooting.

Take the liquor out the hand

of that unpredictable man.

Put some sympathy in the artist

who never thanked that one loyal fan.

The teen with no money

to further their education.

Give him money and self-esteem

to enjoy life's sensations.

The puppy with no eye
resulting from a dog fight.
In your heart you know its wrong-
put some affection in your life.

Find a cure for AIDS
for those infected by their partner.
Just because the partner didn't confess
doesn't mean the victim should suffer.

Stitch the broken heart together
of the girl who was cheated on.
Heal the bruises of the boy-
the one who's constantly beaten on.

Bring back the buildings
destroyed from September 11.
Heal the hearts of the families
who lost their loved ones on Titanic.

Congratulate the single mother
who raised four children.
Give opportunity to the woman
who can't have any.

Those who are mentally challenged
aren't just mentally challenged.
The most underestimated people
can move mountains.

Put the sound in the ears
of that person that can't hear.
Put the vision in the woman
who has dreamed of being something.

Become the change in me
as I become the difference in you.
We can change the world-
just us two.

Never Met Me

You intrude into my presence

as my mind is under tension.

Inconsistent with persistence

you bury me like a victim.

You can't feed me-

let's face it, you don't need me.

There is no truth,

you simply don't see me.

Predictions of how I contradict-

thinking too hard, losing my consciousness.

Emotions don't mean anything-

they fall into a bottomless pit.

Am I sick of it?

No need to ask-

you can see my illustrations,

just read the book of my past.

And time keeps on saying

life is moving too fast.

So I put my car in neutral

just to see if I crash.

Brains on the dash-

thoughts don't even last.

Just get the broom and dust pan

and sweep away like trash.

You don't know me-

this I know.

How am I so certain?

Your actions show.

They show like nudeness,
sometimes I see it as rudeness.
Like I didn't hear you say that-
like I just don't exist.

Feeling the blood rush
through the veins in my wrist.
Communicating with my tolerance
I simply ball my fist.

Trying to figure out
the answer to this.
How can one aim so high
but always seem to miss?

Miss like Mr. and Mrs.-
no hugs and no kiss.
That stone cold love,
stiff like stacked bricks

You can't know me
if you never met my soul.
To judge me by my cover
is to choose the wrong road.

To think I complain for no reason
does that really make sense?
Put on my shoes, make sure you tie them-
now kick yourself some sense.

Is there a such thing as to
aim too high?
I was always taught
to reach for the sky.

So why, why when I-
give my heart and I try-
the sea seems to part
and rain falls from the sky?

As if friendships aren't deceitful
and relationships aren't hard to find.
Like life isn't hard
and love is not blind.

Well if I said that
I think I'd be lying.
My watch must be broken
I've lost track of time, countless times.

And it seems as if I sometimes
exchange words with myself.
Like I have four ears
and I'm just hearing myself.

Talking to myself
as if the person next to me is deaf.
Playing my own melody
without the treble and clef.

Different because I chose to-

foolishly I chose you.

Wondering why we split?

Something told me I was supposed to.

This is not the same

I want the old you.

Maybe it was my mistake,

maybe I didn't really know you.

Now days, a green light means stop

and so does the red ones.

You easily become a victim

and you only live once.

They say don't cry over spoiled milk

but sometimes the drama, it spoils you.

Kills you silently

as it quickly destroys you.

You may ask who do I run to
when I need honest love?
I tell them, if it's not my pencil and paper
Then my best friend is my blood.

No need to mention the name,
they should know who they are.
Only one person stood by me faithfully
through all of this.

I'm not speaking about family-
lord knows I love my real family.
Do anything for them
because my family helped brand me.

I'm standing on the mound
looking down to the ground.
The sand is trying to send a message-
it's trying to tell me to smile.

So it's ironic-

truth is, my smile is beautiful.

But life gets to your head

Please understand what it can do to you.

I love to smile

I refuse to hide my pride.

So if life is a pool-

then I'm a diver, I'll dive.

Sick of lies

Sick of trying

Sick of pain

No time for crying

Knew it wouldn't be easy

but why is it so hard?

Why pretend to be-

why bring me harm?

So when I put up my arms
and seem so aggressive-
It's only normal to me
It means I've learned my lesson.

If you can't respect the fact that
I must stand on my own.
Then please, be my guest
leave me the hell alone

I can't take it easy
I must speak my mind.
You won't take advantage of me
you're wasting time trying.

Never met me
never kept me.
Try not to let a waste of time
reflect or stress me.

You don't see what I see-

you hardly listen to me.

So what I think of you?

Is that you never met me!

Chapter 2: Skin Deep

"Look into the ears and listen to the eyes.

Then you will see past the disguise."

God Iz

A force stronger than any-

yet we often underestimate it.

We lose a little bit in life-

And assume we are devastated.

Look yourself in the eyes

and pay attention to the pain.

The main reason that it's there-

is because you put yourSELF through strain.

No one said it would be easy

but he DID say believe.

And if it wasn't for Him-

how could you possibly breath.

We receive all of the riches-

yet we lack to say thank you.

The only reason I said WE

is because we ALL are in danger.

Romans 8:31

the reading I keep close at heart.

If God be for us-

Who can be against us?

But it is sad to say-

we often push God away.

As if we can make it on our own

Never make time to pray.

So we complain

and become ungrateful when we fall.

Foolishly we miss the point-

of how we made our own call.

It takes a woman to admit wrong-

and a man to do the same.

It takes a child of God to repent-

and change their filthy ways.

It is clear that none of us are
perfect.
But to live ungratefully-
it is never worth it.

God iz the magnificent-
the creator of it all.
If he wanted to, remember-
He could destroy it all.

Too hold your head
and walk tall.
Life by faith,
Not hatred.

Kneel on both knees-
until you feel them start to buckle.
Force your hands together
as if they are stuck like glue.

If you don't do it too often-
then now it is the time to.
There is no limit to the blessings
God will give to you.

And we wonder why the world
has so much drama.
The same reason
you forget to pray.

Prayer brings chance and hope-
and if you think He doesn't answer prayers
Well guess again.
God works in the most unthinkable ways.

And just because you didn't
receive help right away-
doesn't mean that
you've been forgotten.

It simply means that-

not everything you ask for

is good for you.

Let God work his miracles.

Tell me what God does not do

and I'll tell you what He does do.

Tell me that your alone-

I'll say God is watching you.

It's not about who God

is not.

It's about whom

God Iz.

She Cried Herself

There once was a little girl

who cried herself to sleep.

Who cried herself to sleep

because she had nothing to eat.

Who cried herself to sleep

because she had nothing on her feet.

Who cried herself to sleep

because of her irregular heartbeat.

Who cried herself to sleep

because she didn't know-

why oh why, her mother jumped out a window.

Who cried herself to sleep

because she felt alone.

Who cried herself to sleep

because she had no home.

Her deepest fear was not

that she had no home.

But because she was a little girl

having to make it on her own.

The Boy

The cries of a little boy unheard-
you hear the singing of a bird.
He walks, but still can't find-
the monsters, demons in his mind.
The deep emotions in his heart
is the way he felt from the start.

You hear his heart beat, beating fast-
carrying crazy things from his past.
Like, why he fell and slipped on glass.

The blood as it slid down his face-
feeling pain in his eyes like he was sprayed with mace.
He gets up, but at a slow pace-
catching his breath, there was no trace.

He sat there on the floor, dying-
trying to turn back the hands of time.
Crying as blood ran down his eyes-
trying to remember the last fun he had.

The truth which laid dead inside of him-
the pain he held inside.
Wanting to tell someone of his secret-
but they got left behind.
As he moved on forever more-
his body later found washed up on a shore.
Nobody ever knew of the pain inside-
now it was too late, because the boy had died.

Poetry

Reading through my bleeding words

as if it's on its menstrual cycle.

I got a loud intent

as if I own a motor cycle.

Never a phony or a copy-

bring a stop sign if there is need to stop me.

My poetry burns through paper-

bring out the sun block and block me.

My veins are poisoned

with my lyrical content.

I inhale polluted air

and there is no escape vent.

So when they ask me what is poetry-

I shed some blood so they can see

that poetry is every tear

that I ever shed.

It is

every pool that I have ever bleed.

Every smile that I've broken,

and every path that I've chosen.

Poetry is the air I breath

and the sky I see.

The danger that creeps

and the words I speak.

I am poetry.

Her vs. Me

You will never be anything,

you're a mistake to history.

You can talk all you want-

I won't let you get to me.

Then stop writing,

your just scared.

I walk my own path-

You can't compare.

Your path is full of broken ground-

you say you walk tall, but soon you'll fall.

Every word you speak bothers me?

Not at all.

Your father even neglected you,

so what makes you think your special?

I was put on this earth for a reason-

I'm confident, I will succeed.

Your skin is brown and so are your eyes-
the color of dirt, why show some pride?
Why should I hide, I'm a treasure inside-
my skin is rich, I claim all of this.

    Your nothing to them
    and nothing to me.
    That's just your opinion
    I still will be me.

    Keep going you'll see
    that you want to be me.
    I want to be myself,
    so no need to repeat.

Your flesh and your blood
is dying of infection.
I'm not dying, I'm living-
living for a lesson, not perfection.

Who do you think you are?
A human with no heart.
Judging me makes you real?
That's just how you feel.

I hate you, you make life hard-
with you in my life, I'll never go far.
I'm not the problem-
he problem here is you.

Blame me for your mess,
but you're a part of me too!
I am no form of you-
I am better than you.

Your better than me?
Be better than you!
You can't destroy me-
I challenge you to.

That was never my intention-
your mind is slipping.
I'm just fine
but I'm sick and tired of your lies.

I'll continue to talk
until you hear my cries.
Stop ignoring the truth
and open your eyes.

I was never blind-
you made me this way.
Then just end it right now
and kill me today.

I don't want to kill you-
I never meant to cause you pain.
You talk down on me-
poisoning my brain.

I'm done, that's it-

I'll pull the trigger quick.

I'll help you pull it-

BANG!!! Click Click

After Math

After the math

do you add

or subtract life?

Do you multiply vision?

Divide the sense of hearing?

After the math

What's the square root

of a tragedy?

After the math where will you be?

After the grave is made

in a dead end

that you paved.

Flesh ripping like shredded paper,

not even a band-aid could save her.

After the math

Like a needle in the hay stack-
this is a deadly payback.
No eye could make contact.

Brain dead
like it was an overdose.
She just wanted to hold her close.

Sharp pains pierced her heart-
coldly, she was lonely.
Screaming "save me".

Drunk driver smoothly passed by her-
they are liars and innocent she was.
Now she's in furious fires.

Nothings the same.
People crowd and laugh out loud-
emotions in the air like a projectile.

After the math

do you frown

or smile?

There is no outlet-

no plug to pull.

Drowning in sorrow after the math.

After the math

How do you find the path?

Strangled by your own wrath.

How do you read the signs

when your partially blind?

It's just a waste of time.

Her mother has never felt

such an absence

EVER

All she does is shed tears.

Reality knows her baby is gone

FOREVER.

What's a negative

plus a positive

after the math?

Each point is a lead-

connect them

and create a graph.

Turn the graph

into your personal map.

After the math

If ten minus eight

is a solution of two,

subtract one more and there stands you.

After the math

what do you do-

when you lose that someone

who meant the world to you?

Drowning

Struggle, what does that mean?

Not even I can give an example.

I drown in tears

for that child who has the

shape of a lamp pole.

Eyes bloodshot red

with no education in his head.

Brain cells dead.

He'd rather be overfed.

Drowning

Not in a pool of water,

but in a pool of tears.

Tears that have dried up

over all the years.

Tears

Sliding down his face-

his dreams are nightmares.

He just wants to erase

and dream of another place.

Place

That he was born-

left him sick and torn.

He had been used

and watched by many like porn.

Drowning

It may be funny to you,

but it's not funny to me.

Could you live with no

shoes on your feet?

Drowning

No one to talk to-
a very lonely world.
Only blanket he has
is the tail of a squirrel.
Drowning

Not in a bank of water,
but in a field of pain.
Nowhere to turn
and no plug for the drain.
Drowning

Waiting for the pressure
to suffocate you no more.
Even on cold nights
he wishes he had a torch.
Drowning

Where it's even hard

to walk by faith.

He's down on his knees

every day as he prays.

Drowning

Until he can't breathe any more-

until his heart fails

and he can't see any more.

Until he's gone forever

and he can't drown any more.

Elevation Deflation

Higher and higher I reach.

My friends need advice

so I teach.

As I climb these mountains

I feel a tug on my leg.

Underachievers try to pull me down.

I walk with my head high.

The only thing above me

is the sky.

Confident that I make a difference

to all who down me.

I give you forgiveness.

Never the senseless-

around the world like the Census.

To spread the truth is my mission.

The same people I grew up with
I've seen them coming down-
tumbling like leaves to the ground.

So many traps and dead ends
try to hold me at point blank.
But I can't stop, I must rank.

The elevation to my success-
the biggest needle couldn't deflate that.
I won't let it.

Sometimes life is like a firefly
and you can't catch it.
Like a hit man, a hidden message.

Pay attention-
open your eyes and listen.
Give yourself definition.

Not so much to be conceited,

but to trust in yourself-

you need it!

So what's my level of elevation?

I'm reaching high-

I'm sky scraping.

If I shall fall

I must get back up.

A true heart couldn't try too much.

What is success?

What's determination?

There is no meaning without cooperation.

So what's my level of elevation?

I'm reaching high.

I'm sky scraping.

I Stand

Grew up on Chicago's south side-

drugs and gang wars did not hide.

The only girl, raised with three boys.

So I was taught to be aggressive

and never to be influenced by the negative noise.

Eventually daddy gave up.

I was about thirteen,

I'm thinking "dude man up".

If they would ask me was my father great-

I would not put my hand up.

He was there until I became a teen,

but after that he started lying-

saying things he didn't mean.

Turning broken promises into false dreams-

and this is who helped birth me?

I'm older now and I kick at his dirt-

what is it worth?

Nothing at all, he hasn't seen my progress.

Very successful, the opposite of him.

It's funny how this guy is a part of my rib.

Mother so independent-

spoiled me with her blessings.

Even when we get into it

I know somewhere there is a message.

It's up to me to catch it.

I refuse to end up

like some of my drunk uncles

and aunts.

I was raised on better grounds-

I must take what I want.

It's time for me to stand!

Even if I'm alone, I'll wear the pants.

I raise my hand.

I'm a part of the stronger brand

as I STAND.

Grandma

In my best friend's dorm room

is where I was when I received the call.

I heard the words clearly

but I didn't want to read the writings on the wall.

Mother was telling me

that my grandma had just passed.

That very moment, it feels like

I hopped on a plane, and it crashed.

Thinking too fast because I was so confused-

a college student on the run, an overload to my shoes.

My eyes couldn't help it, they had to cry.

Suddenly I stopped, and whipped the tears from my eyes.

Heartbroken because she's my second mother-

took care of me as a child, never let me suffer.

My grandma is a blessing-

how can I not I love her?

It hurt my heart just to look at her
in those hospital beds, band-aids, and needles.
Too much pain, looking at her like
grandma please maintain.

I saw it in her eyes
and she didn't want to go through it.
So I cried inside for her-
deep inside we all knew it.

I call her *Gun-Ga-*
that name came from my baby days.
And thanks to support from my grandma
I'd say I am well raised.

An aggressive woman she was,
but still sweet at heart.
My grandma is my angel
and my masterpiece of art.

And when I look at my life
she plays a huge role in it.
She was always the father in my life
whenever my daddy wasn't in it.

I wouldn't be who I am
if not for my grandma and mother.
Even through arguments
we still loved each other.

My tears will dry up
but my love for my grandma will never perish.
She taught me how to stay strong-
her wisdom I truly cherish.

I can never forget the memories-
they are a part of me.
Forgetting a thing like that-
would be to erase me.

She'd do anything for me
and that is a fact.
Whenever I had problems-
grandma always had my back.

They say a big star appeared in the skies
the night God took her away.
It was a sign to all of us-
God needed her more than we.

Cause now she can watch over us-
Lord knows how much I'll miss her.
One day I'll wake up
and plan to go visit and kiss her.

But this is a lifetime challenge
and she'd only want me to be strong.
So I will take my family's hand
and tell them to hold on.

My grandma is my flesh-
my grandma is my bone.
Grandma helped make me a woman-
she wants me to move on.

So no matter how hard
that this challenge may be-
I know I can do it
because my grandma see's it in me.

I saw it in her and now my grandma is free.
She'll always hold my hand, she'll help me succeed.
A strong black female, yes that's what I call her.
I will be proud to tell my future children all about her.

If I see her in the mirror
as I wash my soft face-
I know she's smiling back at me,
taking my heart to embrace.

No need to stay on this earth-
we all know it's hell.
But I looked up to my grandma
and told her I will not fail.

And as the years go by
I may shed a few tears.
Reminding myself
of all the past years.

But we cannot prevail
if we don't forgive our past.
And even the best things in life
won't always last.

I look at the road ahead
and I must go straight.
Even when the devil tells me
"don't concentrate."

I will continue to be
who my grandma helped create.
Those who have not been there
can't relate.

I put chances with opportunities
and take my place.
And look heaven in the eye
with a smile on my face.

And if someone asks me
how long has she been gone?
I'll say "my grandma didn't leave,
she was just never at home."

So I look at her and say, THANK YOU-
blessed with your love, I am THANKFUL.
Always and forever
I will miss you.

Damaged

A prisoner in my own body-

internally bleeding.

Heart bruised from being accused-

your suspect, so you lose.

When tears get loose

they don't even drop.

They evaporate half way down your face

and leave you in awe.

You bleed through your thoughts-

your burning inside like hot sauce.

So you're ready to ball up-

like fresh fruit with the top off.

They say you can't fix a failure,

but I say they are all story tellers.

Because to them you're another black person.

Another skillful artist trying to paint the picture perfect.

Don't become what they label you-
then see what they will say to you.
Because either way, someone will have something to say
like they created you.

Don't wear your heart on your sleeve
and don't let the world tease.
This will only make you weak-
they will become the air you breathe.

Polluted and toxicated-
they will say you'll never make it.
Better wear some better shoes
and be sure to switch your pace up.

No stitches or band-aids-
just let the cuts burn.
Because you're strong, they'll find out
that damage doesn't last too long.

To Speak

To speak is for me to part thy lips

and open thy mind.

For I speak not of uncertainty,

but by what is trapped inside waiting to escape.

Beating at my chest like a locked up ape.

I am not my ass, and I am not my breast.

If that is all you see in me, then look at me less.

For I will pay you no attention, for you do not deserve to take my breath away.

I don't have to settle for it.

It's a price I refuse to pay!

Why is it that every word that escapes from a male's mouth is either bitch, trick, or hoe?

Ladies we are only what we respond to, so let these guys know.

I stand for thy honestly, thy love, and thy loyalty.

Too many times I've been lied to as these people try to ruin me.

I look lies in the eye, and tell them YOUR NOT SHIT.

Please excuse my language, but they asked for it.

I have a mouth to speak, so when needed I use it.

They don't know the meaning of dedication.

They just want to give up, very little patient.

I am speaking about relationships-

they'd rather go find a girl with those loose lips.

I am not speaking of the mouth-

I'm speaking of them girls who go from house to house.

That's what these guys are all about.

They too stuck on bullshit, that they'll never find real out.

So your thinking what is this about?

I'm tired of repeating myself, you know my story.

I don't go for dudes who smoke, and drink up their life like it's important.

And if you want me because of sex, then forget it, go fuck another.

I'm not about to sit around and be your next baby's mother.

I'm looking for a lover, someone who's dedicated.

And when the stairs get slippery, they still get elevated.

You can hate, take it how you please.

But I bet when I meet a real man, he will be very pleased.

Pleased that I am the type he had to fight for.

Knew he had to be persistent in order to open doors.

And he is going places, and he doesn't represent any gangs.

He wants to make a difference, and that's why I got his last name.

Real

Living life as a young lady-

where many dudes tried to play me.

I looked them dead in the eye and said "you can just hate me."

As they mentally tried to rape me

I sat back contemplating.

Picture the venomous mind of a poet-

my lyrics speak for their self - pressure of a gun

as I cock back, squeeze, and reload it.

You asking for pain

I'll let you hold it.

My pencil writing so deep

that the crease in the paper has it folded.

Evicted like an apartment notice-

my mind is irritated by the noise, like a locus.

Lady Poet, I must stay focused-

I'm through playing cards with them jokers.

Throwing chips like its poker-

I'm polluted like a smoker.

Too many immature minds

It's like I'm pushing a baby stroller.

The world is slowly dying!

Where is hell? We are. living in it

We are so blind to the obvious!

Why can't we pay attention?

My words are my mission-

I'm fishing for permission.

So unsure of our own, we fall for contradiction-

an overdose and addiction.

Stuck in neutral, time to buy a new transmission-

I'm sick of looking through my soul

just to dream of me wishing-

that I can bring smiles upon the faces of those who are in poverty.

Don't touch me, don't bother me-

I'm on my own, I got to see.

Be a leader, a prophecy-

my footsteps, come follow me.

See my poetry has a mind of its own.

My poetry isn't newborn-

its truthfully full grown.

It can stand on its own-

through the flesh of my bone.

Ladies just be ladies-

never settle for foul movement.

If it doesn't add up, then it's time for improvement-

hallucinations and illusions.

Better pick the road you're cruising-

end up on the rebound, like a plumber with his tool kit.

The foolishness needs to stop!

Life is too short to live your life, stumbling over rocks.

And if poetry is marijuana,

then I'm smoking a blunt.

I'm running after mine, like a football punt.

As I get high off the aroma

and pass out in my coma-

I look down at this world

and watch it go under.

Trading Places

I wonder what life would be like
if I just traded places.
Trades places with who?
Trade places with you.

You could walk in my shoes-
that's if the shoe fits.
And we could build from there
with multiple sticks.

I'd like to take the journey
to experience you.
It is a dangerous challenge-
would you experience me too?

I know I'd be taking risks
but I am ready.
Let's just trade places-
different lives, different settings.

See I'm known for having
very stylish shoes.
But when I put my feet in-
I sometimes catch the blues.

Sometimes I even lose-
when it's up to me to choose.
A corruption to myself-
as if my screws have been stripped.

Let's trade places.
No, I'm not complaining-
cause the life that I live
is quite fascinating.

But I want you to see
the softer side of me.
The non-hardcore side-
the side that's usually more weak.

So if we can't trade places-
next time look and see.
That when I open my eyes-
catch a glimpse of me.

Not my eyes, but me!
Look inside and see.
I shine like a new car-
but I can come down like a tree.

Reach for me-
put your hand through my soul.
Blow air into my lungs
And be the warmth to my cold.

And when you have me in your hand-
please don't close it.
Communicate with me-
leave the door to your heart open.

And I will do the same for you-
if you need me to.
You can be the eyes for me-
and I'll be the eyes for you.

Now what is it like
when you wear a mismatch shoe?
Does it mean your half of me
and that I'm a half of you?

Let's think about this-
will trading places make us happy?
Knowing we ran away from fear
and that we gave up on ourselves?

Let's NOT trade places-
lets create a legacy.
I'll help you take the steps-
a leg for you, a leg for me.

You're a Liar

Women can't take pain?

You're a liar.

What do you call it every month

when we survive the fire?

Give us respect-

we're tired.

But I'm laughing because you're crazy.

You wouldn't even be here, thank a lady.

The thought of a living thing

being forced out of your womb.

It's like attempting to comb nappy hair

with a toothless comb.

My obligation

is to spread the correct information.

It takes patience-

plus a lot of consideration.

Too many times do we waste time-
attempting to climb the grape vine.
Looking for a fresh grape-
but end up with sour wine.

Nasty taste left on the tongue-
Swallowing stupidity.
know your own worth-
Never lose your dignity.

He's a liar if he says
you'll never make it!
But your just as foolish as he
if you confirm the point he's making.

Being a woman is a fulltime job
and even when it's hard-
Look forward
with no regards.

Let them all

continue to be liars.

When he comes running back-

Tell him YOU A LIAR!

Self-Contradiction

In the green zone-

voices in my head ringing like a ringtone.

I'm feeling myself, literally-

flesh and bone.

Not angry, but in my eyes I see anger-

reflections in the mirror

personally looking at a stranger.

You think you know me?

Obviously you've fallen into a perception

of my self-neglecting.

While looking upon my existence-

a self detection.

Memorizing the stupidity!

My conscience is nonsense-

so when I write, you read my memory.

Not that any of it matters-
cause at the end of the frame
I still hear the people chatter.
So I silently disregard all of my-
my lost words at heart.
As if life isn't hard, like life has no heart.

Never said I meant to-
since everything is mental
I spread my thoughts on the line
and give birth to a pencil.
Out the womb comes every shattered tear.
Every painful thought, thirsty , a can of beer.

Not that it tastes good
because it burns my tongue.
And I've already died-
speaking from my lungs.
Hungry because I ate my power-
no longer an opportunity.
That's because my existence
pours of sour.

Just listen, speaking isn't enough-
like I'm not good enough.
Life, just give it up.
Scuffed like new Nikes-
laced with no strings.
Falling out of the shoe
like a bird with no wings.

My words have no means-

my purpose has no dreams.

By the time she figures it out-

realize what every word means.

She will never understand me-

I give it up, I guess I'm stuck.

Suspect

I overheard the whole conversation-
the two people were communicating
then they both started debating.

He said the suspect is too aggressive
and that she needs to fix herself up.
And that moment I wanted to slap him
and tell him to shut the hell up.

He started saying she was worthless
and that she was a waste of time.
He said she had no potential
and that she was clearly blind.

Without a doubt in my mind
I would think that he was crazy.
But I went pitch black
because my mind became hazy.

Stuttering by the mouth, he stood up

and banged on the table.

He started ripping up paper and calling

her out her name.

I laughed

I laughed so hard

that I remembered he was childish.

So I also stood up

and decided to end this.

Every word from my mouth

split my tongue in half.

I was piercing him with my mind-

ready to give him a blood bath.

I laughed

I remembered not to let him get the

best of me.

It was obvious-

he was simply testing me.

So he got angry and asked

why I was laughing?

I laughed

I said your actions speak

and reveal who you are.

How dare you speak down on another

when your self-ill.

Need a self check, as well as some respect.

But if you want to stay on that path

God will give you a rain check.

So he stood there

looking all rejected.

I laughed

Now whose suspect?!

Daddy

The perfect example of what a man is NOT.

You're a child in the frame of a man.

It's sad to say, but it's the truth-

all you do is lie and pretend.

Will you ever play your part?

You shouldn't start what you can't finish.

Your hardly involved in anything I do-

do yourself a favor and vanish.

Luckily I have the greatest mother-

who has helped me achieve so much.

Daddy is just an alcoholic

who pays more attention to Corona than us.

I've lost respect for you-

what more do you expect.

It's about time you man up-

I carry a bigger heart than you.

Lie after lie-
I get sick of the bull.
I don't even listen anymore-
It's like talking to a fool.

When I was little-
you always made time.
Now I'm years older
and you act as if time doesn't exist.

I must keep it real with you
just so you can see.
I just don't understand
because it took TWO to make me.

Mother did this
and mother did that.
There were times when I had to say
"mother just relax."

Now you've turned me against you-
you no longer hold the title.
You don't even ask how I'm doing in school.
What type of father are you?

The drinking will catch up to you-
and the smoking will add on to that.
There will be no way for me to save you-
as if you deserved that.

The apologies you've given me
are never the truth.
You say sorry
then do the same thing times two.

The tables have turned-
I'm older now.
You can't even keep a real woman
and I see how.

You motivate me to do better.

Each and every one

of your short comings

serve as an example.

So thanks daddy, for making me stronger.

I do not hate you!

You're simply just another average black father.

I will make my life successful

rather your involved in it or not.

And if you ever decide to actually play your role-

give it your BEST shot.

Don't Let Go

You can make it if you try-

wipe the tears from your eyes.

Do not settle for less-

your priceless, be yourself.

You don't need all of the pain-

stand tall and defeat the storm.

They'll try and hate you-

but that doesn't mean to let them stop you.

To all my single mothers

you can do it without him-

raise beautiful children.

They grow up to be a blessing

and the world can admire them.

To all my pregnant ladies-

so young, I'm talking babies having babies.

Slow down, you have plenty of time to grow-

You're not ready for a child, you just THINK so.

To all of the faithful husbands

don't get distracted.

The women in tight clothes

want your attention, but their only acting.

It's not worth it when you've got a great wife at home.

Love your children, even when they become full grown.

To all my rape victims

I pour out my heart for you.

He didn't even have a right

to force himself on top of you.

A young mind, you probably didn't even know what hit you-

when he repeatedly forced his penis

through every virgin tissue.

To everyone in the army, navy, and more

I give honor to you.

Although some could care less

if you live or die-

I see the entire struggle

through the pain you fight.

To all the alcoholics and drug abusers

what will your children think of you?

Or even a nephew or niece!

What will you do when they see what you do

and try it?

You can't even get mad, because you didn't try to hide it-

you didn't try to fight it.

All you did was swallow and puff.

I guess your last heart attack wasn't warning enough.

To all the children in other countries

who die from lack of food-

I give all I can give

to help you make it through.

People laugh at the famine

like it's all a big joke.

Soon they will laugh too hard-

and choke.

To all the police officers

as much as I'd love to hate you.

You've helped with so much-

I guess I'm saying THANK YOU.

I understand that usually

your only doing your job.

And sometimes even we citizens make that hard.

To all the thugs-

what advantage does "thug life" really get you?

Only a new suit and a casket.

Is it worth it just to die over a color?

Or shoot up a neighborhood, killing someone's little brother.

Is it worth it in the end

to end up in jail?

Sitting in a dirty cell-

like your rotting in hell.

To all the great and deceased

you were a present here on earth.

You put in hard time and dedication

so younger generations could grow.

This here is not a letter
and it is not just a poem.
It's a message to everyone
who feels like losing hope.
Hold tight
and don't let go of the rope.

Have faith in yourself
and believe in your heart.
If you can't finish the battle
then don't try to start.
Don't let go of your future
and learn from your past.
Make a decision-
make a difference.
This is the power YOU have.

I Am Me

I am who I am-
different perspectives I see.
So I don't get mad anymore
when people envy me.

I won't change for anyone
because change doesn't change for me.
Look into my soul-
tell me what you see.

Don't look with your ears-
people gossip all the time.
Don't judge by the cover-
Focus on the inside.

If you must hate me-
then you hate me for being real.
I am who I am-
this is only a part of how I feel.

My brown skin protects me

from any unknown germ.

It protects my heart

so that my mind can learn.

My emotions are not a game-

neither is it a puzzle.

That's why people don't understand

the true meaning of "I Love You."

I am loved by few-

and hated on by many.

But at the end of the day

I've inspired plenty.

The hate that I encounter-

I use it as fuel.

It motivates me to succeed-

teaches me to keep my cool.

You can hate me all you want

but don't push me.

I stand my own grounds-

looking up to NO "bully".

To get my respect

you must earn it,

Life is not how you take it

but instead how you live it.

Failure is not an option

Success is the key.

I plan to open every door-

letting no one stop me.

They try to block my paths

they'll see.

It's like a battlefield with me.

I'll crush every dream you ever had

that was about defeating me.

A beast is what you see-
sometimes it's what I have to be.
So that trouble makers and haters
won't try and run through me.

I inspire you to be yourself-
happiness starts within the soul.
I know who I was
and I know who I am.
I am me, and nobody else.

Beautiful Black Woman

Beautiful black woman
you have come so far.
In the eyes of some, you don't count-
in the eyes of many, you're a star.

You've held the egg
of a blessed creation.
Taken the beating
over decades and generations.

Beautiful black woman
do not be ashamed.
Though some misuse your name-
knocking down your frame.

Thick and healthy thighs-
white and sexy teeth.
Hips that present many curves
and eyes that tell a story.

You're not just ordinary-

you're a landmark in history.

Because of the struggle you had

life is better for me.

As a beautiful black woman myself-

I give credit to all my black woman.

For every struggle-

every tear.

Men treat us as an underdog

like were less of importance.

They even refuse to take care of their children-

forcing some of us to take an abortion.

They don't understand the pain-

the kicking, the screaming.

The yelling from abusive husbands-

the stress, the beatings.

They don't give you credit
for everything that you've improved.
The mountains that you've climbed
and the oceans that you've moved.

Beautiful black woman
Stand up for your rights.
Even if it means to bleed-
even if it means to fight.

For every great woman
comes great challenges.
From every struggle
there is a gain.

For every lock
there is a key.
For every flood
there is a drain.

Beautiful black woman

don't let the world look down on you.

They judge by contact

I bet they haven't walked in your shoes.

Beautiful black woman.

Theme for English 3

The professor said,

"Go home and write

a page tonight.

And let that page come out of you-

Then, it will be true."

I wish it was that simple.

I am a young female,

born on the south side of Chicago.

My eyes cry for America,

but they don't see my heart though.

As I write this paper

I let my pen cry.

It's written so much,

that the ink has went dry.

Some look at a female
and assume that she can't
compare to the strengths of a man.
But women have created wonders,
with her bare hands.
Great things that changed America-
some even a man can't comprehend.

My pen is still crying-
now the paper is drenched.
The smell is tremendous-
I'll get sick off the stench.

Then look at all the teens
who smoke and rush to have sex.
All it takes is one mistake-
what's the advantages of that?

My heart slowly dies

for every abandoned child.

The hope that I have for these children

is the only thing holding my smile.

My pen is finally dying

because it wants America to see.

That behind this pen and paper-

the tears came from me.

This is my page for English 3

Like A Racecar

What if you were born as a racecar?

Wheels raggedy and torn.

Body black and smooth-

eyes constantly rained on.

Sometimes you face situations

that turn into a problem.

So you sit in your garage-

the warmth makes you feel like a model.

You're almost out of oil-

a sign of neglect.

You've been filthy for months-

so your paint doesn't reflect.

Your weakest part is your body-

caused by so many accidents.

Your driver doesn't like to be seen-

so he likes his window tint.

Your heart is not healthy-
I call it your engine.
Even your ignition is broken-
there is a key stuck in it.

Your tired of being the underdog-
your emotions are smashed.
You've tried your hardest
but still you finish last.

It's the last race-
moving at a fast pace.
He presses on the gas-
not knowing he has no brakes.

Neglect of perfection-
he tries to slow it down.
Your heart breaks in two
and you can't even speak now.

The car won't make a sound-

the driver is alright now.

The racecar is totaled-

no reason to fight now.

Try

If words do not come out

then how am I speaking?

If I am tired for twenty four hours

then I must not be sleeping.

If the kitchen is invaded with crumbs

it means I'm not sweeping.

How can I be emotional-

when I'm not even weeping?

How can I inspire many

if yet I have to inspire one?

How can you want to succeed

when your life revolves around guns?

Failure is not an option-

but neither is success.

If you give up all the time

and never try your best.

Blocks, rocks, sticks, stones

will not break you.

Unless you let it-

but at the same time, don't be selfish.

How can I swim

without proper skill?

If unskilled hands can shoot guns-

what's the deal?

You only fail if you don't try-

so can you try and not fail?

Can you walk on top of water?

No, but you can still ascend the stairs.

Voice Yourself

Mouth wide open-

No lyrics

Beautiful personality-

No spirit

Tear drops on your face-

No feelings

Cement and construction-

No building

Movement is fluent-

Like water over rocks

Mind so confused-

A crooked cop

No one can see you-

Invisible

Each of your actions

Predictable

Choice

Minus the CH

Replaced-

V

Voice yourself

Sometimes

Sometimes I feel misplaced-
like a runaway child.
I'd like to be cared for
but I haven't known love for a while.

Sometimes I just want to cry-
but my heart won't let it flow.
I try to stay positive-
I don't want the pain to show.

Sometimes my heart leaks-
I think I'm running out of time.
Pain will leave you scarred-
it left me deaf and blind.

I don't know how to fix this-
I think I'm a little too late.
I don't understand the pressure-
so I blame myself with hate.

Sometimes I wonder why
I go through so much.
I've done nothing to anyone
except provide everlasting love.

Sometimes I wonder if
someone understands my pain.
Have they been through the fire-
Gotten burned by the flames.

Sometimes I go to sleep
hoping for a better day.
Then again sometimes I wish-
these time would go away.

Slaves No More

Beautiful black ladies and gents

we are slaves no more.

You no longer have to suffer-

nor go through the back door.

No more holding your mind in rage-

you have strength to turn the page.

No more starving for days-

nor in the fields, scorched by rays.

Memories from deep in the past-

beat us until our red flesh shown.

Still they didn't brak us all-

we showed them how we glow.

Tortured us like a helpless animal-

tried to eat us alive like a cannibal.

Handled us black women like a tool-

used us, threw us away, then buried us.

It's scary isn't it, because we make differences-
We are slaves no more, learn from it.
Repeatedly raped our women-
then used the baby as labor.

They sold us off like cattle-
Their favorite phrase was "pay us".
Yet we still haven't learned-
we still enslave ourselves daily.

We are at war with ourselves-
the white men doesn't need to kill us.
We keep killing ourselves-
Self-prejudice.

We steady hate each other-
when we need to work together.
We constantly fail ourselves-
how can we ever get better?

We throw our knowledge down the drain-

like spoiled food in the sink.

Too busy following trends-

buying chinchillas and minks.

The media already puts a label on us-

but then again, these are things we enforce.

We keep building the track-

but we never finish the course.

We are slaves no more-

so we need to act like it.

We are our own enemy-

Time to work that black magic.

The Title

Broken mirror pieces-
sharp and dangerous edges.
Paper shredding on the black top.
Moisture in the eye of the beholder.

Who are you to judge he?
You are not thee!
No meaning at all
to a word that you speak.

I see he, literally I do!
Who is she to me?
Who is she to you?
Who, Who, Who?

Her other support vanished-
selfishness is not success.
There is a million in the crowd-
she is not like the rest.

Sin after sin-

why betray yourself?

Hand by hand-

will make you murder yourself.

Don't close the door-

yet, she is trying.

A face with many faces-

but her heart is drowning.

Hammer and nail, pounding-

speakers and music, sounding.

One step ahead of the game-

then her foot sinks into the quick sand.

Rusty like crust on a pan-

heavy on myself like a bed.

Ruff like rocks in a bag-

hit and run, I hit myself.

Got back up to get messed up-
deep in my system.
Like I'm factory made-
weak, like I came from my grave.

Paved pavement, a replacement-
like dust on the walls in my basement.
African American, but I see Asian-
I'm racing, constantly pacing.

White is the color of angel like memories.
Red is the color of broken images.
Brown is the color of my skin.
Black is the frame they put me in.

Constantly flowing like fluid-
cool me down like coolant.
No gas in my tank
so call me E.

Place the M in the front

and spell out ME.

If that's what you see,

then that's who I be.

The only enemy I have is me!

Not a cry for help, but a plea.

This is who I chose to be.

Deep, but too deep for you to understand.

Read everything on my mind

through the palm of my hand.

Intelligence of the better-

mixed up with the weather.

Hard like a nut

but soft like a feather.

Real like leather-

defeat me, never.

Conquer

A coral reef in the ocean-

loating without notice.

Running into so many currents

that I constantly lose focus.

And I'm hoping that my ocean

doesn't wash me on a shore.

Cause I'd be walked on and stepped on

like a mat at a door.

Am I a trap?

What am I for?

My life I must conquer-

for if I start my own fire

my existence will burn first.

This not a verse.

This is my hearse.

I mean for better or for worse.

I'm too jagged and I snag

like a zipper on a purse.

And I am a part of my intuition.

I have made my decision.

A lady on a mission

to conquer with strong vision.

Testing Me

Waking up in the middle of the night
thinking if I have my head on tight.
Looking myself in the mirror-
a homicide, I pulled the trigger.

Yet that was all in my mind
simply because I've been tested.
No longer have I realized-
everything I have been blessed with.

So I'm thinking-
forget it, I will keep going.
Rain, sleet, snow-
my pen will keep glowing.

As I give birth to the ink on the paper
I realize minutes later
I am not writing on paper-
Just vapor.

Writing this poetry with the contents
my mind thinking.
I'm catching a headache-
I feel my mind bleeding.

Why she keep on testing me?
I don't like this pain.
But I realized in the end-
It was my poetic vein.

Ready to bust
and express itself.
Impatiently waiting
to transform itself.

Too long
I kept it on the shelf
and now it's testing me.

And it will permanently bleed

until the death of me.

No Meaning

There is no meaning to this.

I'm wasting ink and paper.

Just because I want to

jot down how I feel.

My emotions have no meaning either.

No one seems to listen.

I'm invisible

and they don't even see me.

This is pointless-

I'm breathless.

My lips don't move-

I'm faceless.

I've wasted about five minutes now-

I didn't even know I could count.

Of course that doesn't make sense-

none of this does.

I'm the busted tire on the road.

I've been pushed to the side.

I'm not even rubber-

does rubber cry?

This has no meaning!

Why don't you listen?

I'm like a broken glass

in someone's kitchen.

What does it mean to

not have meaning?

In the dictionary under "meaningless"-

you will see me.

This paper isn't real

and neither are these words.

Are you thinking deep enough?

Inside the truth hurts.

If this is pointless

then it wouldn't be here.

But I am here-

can't you see me?

I have legs

but I can't stand.

That doesn't make sense-

I always stand.

I stand

for the right to be me.

I stand for education.

I stand for every child.

I stand for the better-

I'm still standing through the storm.

I stand because if I don't-

who will?

I stand

I stand

I stand

No meaning?

That is ridiculous!

The meaning is deep-

you'll just have to reach!

So when you open the cover

to that big dictionary-

look under the word "stand"

and you will see me.

I stand for whom?

I stand for me!

No meaning does not define me.

It is a phrase that they label me.

I won't sit back

and watch the world trade on me.

I stand for you?

MAYBE

Suicide

Drawing stick figures on the blank sheet

of paper.

I draw a sharp object

of what appeared to be a razor.

I pull the razor out of the paper

and turn it into reality.

I force it to my temple

as if it is a casualty.

Cowardly, I push forcefully

until paper edges fall out of my head,

It didn't take long for me to realize

I had already been dead.

The figures on the paper

had no type of head.

That's when I realized-

the pencil I was writing with

had no type

of lead.

The fantasy I was drawing

was all in my head.

Chapter 3: Love, Lust & Beyond

"Be aware of the thorns, they stare.

But don't miss out on the true flowers that actually care."

Tasty

Strawberry flavored lip gloss on my lips.

Victoria's Secret, seven dollars.

I part my lips to speak to him-

so attractive, perhaps my body became active.

Biting my bottom lip, I slipped up-

I said "hey".

He blessed me with his eyes as he waved.

Feeling myself shiver, I was ready to taste.

My mind was ready to eat up all of his cake-

I had to tell myself wait!

Just take it slow-

but before I could say so,

he walked over and spoke.

He glanced into my eyes-

said I was so beautiful.

I was supposed to say thank you-

but I was in another world.

I could tell he wasn't quite good at this.

He wasn't really the outgoing type.

No ring on his finer-

my eyes told on me, they said

give it to me right.

He smiled, even though I didn't say a word.

I was ready for him to take it-

breakfast, lunch, dinner, and desert!

Yes, he was very appealing-

I was ready to climb his building.

Body rock hard, I had to stop myself from feeling.

Here I go again
playing with my own emotions.
Knowing I didn't really want him
just because I didn't know him.

Perhaps I shall give him an invite-
but before I opened my mouth
he was two inches away from my lips
as he gently held my hips.

I took a big breath,
then I slightly licked my lips.
The sad thing is-
I was still at the table
staring at my empty spoon.

He wasn't anywhere in sight

but I was definitely ready.

Yet I deceived myself, heavy.

I looked at my spoon and laughed-

he must have been TASTY.

Who Do You Tell

Who do you tell

when your emotions take over?

Hoping that someone else

senses the hunger.

Heart so empty

that I need you with me.

I just don't know where to start.

Your touches

your kisses.

Your style-

I miss it.

Our memories-

the friendship.

Did it fall apart?

Who flipped it?

So true

So sweet

What more can I need?

You were there and always there for me.

Who do I tell

when I love someone?

Friends just sometimes never listen-

the touch of your hands all over my face.

Hugging me-

telling me our friendship is great.

But through all the years-

our pain and tears

why did my love for you change?

Silently wishing that you could come get me-

"buddy" I'm not that hard to find.

I want to be yours-

just take over my mind.

I once was told that love is blind.

I go to school

I dream

I sleep

I fantasize

I look into the mirror

and see your pretty eyes.

Do you feel the same way?

I want to hear you say my name.

My past-

I shall not blame.

They say one man's lost

is another man's treasure.

Will I be yours to keep?

We've been friends for years-

shared so many tears.

But together we made it through-

all of a sudden I'm wondering why you took over.

Why am I feeling you?

Usually not the type to hook up with a friend

but I'm lost.

Please hold my hand.

Are you still single?

I am.

You went from a child-

into a strong man.

No, I'm not a fanatic-
I'm just letting you have it.
Boy just come and grab it-
you can be my rabbit.
I'll entertain you like a show on television-
you keep me laughing.
You can be my remote
and control my every move.
Boy keep it real-
you know I want you.

Who do I tell when I love someone?
I'd really rather be your friend-
because with love
comes pain
and with pain
comes rain.
Somebody understand.

No matter what

we will still make things happen.

Who do I tell when I love someone?

I am finally going to tell you the truth.

I love you-

and you said you feel the same?

YES-

thank God for you.

I hope that our love stays true.

Will We Ever

Will we ever have our moment, to shine like a star?

Will we ever have the love, which we once had before?

But before you leave, just let me say goodbye.

All the times I've held you-

after your long days at work.

And the times you told me-

you would always help me cope.

But still I have nothing to say.

Please, why can't you just stay?

The question I asked, I never received an answer.

You left me feeling like a girl with cancer.

I should have been good to you when I had the chance to.

Now I've lost you, what more can I do?

The feeling inside makes me break down and cry.

I'm trying to stay strong, but I can't lie-

I treated you wrong, when I knew you deserved better.

Will we ever kiss again? What about a hug?

What about another romantic night?

When we watched the sunset and birds took flight.

I'm sorry that I didn't pay attention to you-

I guess that is why I surely miss you.

But if I could do it all again, I'd start all over with you as my man.

Love

Where are you love?
I've been searching for you.
I've been stabbed in the heart-
I've been hurting for you.

Where are you love?
Are you born from the womb?
Grow with me, I'm broken-
like the teeth on a comb.

Where are you love?
I've been fighting for you.
People don't believe in you-
I must prove that you are true.

Where are you love?
Are you looking for me?
Are you passionately waiting?
Are you a part of me?

I reach out for you-
yet I can't feel you.
I put my ear towards your heart-
yet I can't hear you.

Are you really there
or just a mist in the night?
I can't prove the people wrong
if you not helping me fight.

Deep like six feet-
I'm talking mountain steep.
Cold like a creek-
warm like the heat.

Where are you love?
My heart is calling.
Like branches in spring time-
I am falling.

When I sleep at night

I dream of me and you.

I contradict myself-

do dreams come true?

These here words are dead-

the thoughts are all in my head.

Without you love, I am nothing.

Just bury me in my bed.

Zoom In

From my scalp

to the roots of my hair.

Deep in the sockets of my eyes

you'll see me stare.

Your tongue moves in waves

as you speak you me.

My mind is confused-

what did you do to me?

Every blood cell

through every stream.

My mouth opens-

I want to scream.

How do I know if

you are here for me?

I expect you to take my eyes out

and blind fold me.

You hear my heart race-

BOOM, BOOM.

The lyrics to my song-

my TUNE, TUNE.

The pieces of flesh-

flesh and bone.

With a caramel type complexion-

you see my tone.

As I touch

your soft hands.

I feel warmth

like a blanket.

When I look in your eyes-

I'm looking at your heart.

I'm concerned that I might-

be ripped apart.

Too deep in it
like I can't walk out.
I want to love you
but I don't know how.

I stare blankly
at what seems to be nothing.
But I am looking at you-
something.

Like I'm driving full speed
right into a brick wall.
That would be a tragic moment
to hear death call.

Holding this pen in my hand-
fingers moist with sweat.
I wipe moisture from my eye-
I'm kind of upset.

Like a reject-
I don't want to try for nothing.
Life down the drain-
like a toilet flushing.

Crushed liked Crush soda-
dangerous like a can opener.
I'm taking a risk gambling
like I'm playing poker.

Look beyond the name
and focus on the skin deep.
Sometimes I despise that
because my skin creeps.

I'm lost in a world
of miserable sacrifice.
And I'm against the odds
like I'm rolling dice.

I can't feel what I see
and I can't hear what I feel.
I'm nine holes deep
like I've been shot with a drill.

The truth is
your just trickery.
You buzz and you sting
just like a bee.

Sorry for me
as if I'm in trouble.
When my lips part-
you expect me to say "I love you."

But something is wrong-
My interior is in need of repair.
My windshield is dirty
but I see crystal clear.

I'm suffocating
and there is no oxygen here.
I throw my hands to the sky
like I'm grabbing for air.

How will I know
if you're the perfect match?
Matches light fires-
why should we toast to that?

Explode to that-
like a bomb threat.
My heart is going down
like the sunset.

Paying attention yet?
I don't expect you to.
I will go and be me
and you can go and be you.

Question is-

who are you?

A shadow on the wall

that I constantly give a name to.

They say the things I say

are very painful.

I tell them that I eat pain

as if it is my brain food.

Zoom in and catch a better picture.

You are stuck to me, like a blister.

This is my final goodbye-

I'll miss you.

Sweet Temptation

I'm walking by myself

as I look your body up and down.

My hormones start talking

every time you come around.

The sight of your lips

make me want to taste.

Movies on playback in my head-

it's hard to stay in place.

Your body has me calling.

I picture you soaking wet.

You all over me-

I often fantasize about that.

If I want you

I can get you.

I'm tempted to let you in-

although that would be a sin.

Your eyes create rivers

below my belt.

I want you to make me scream

like I desperately need help.

Sweet like a box of candy-

hung over you, like I just drank Brandy.

They say look, but don't touch.

But looking isn't enough.

My mind is in a rush-

your essence is too much.

I'd overdose

off of the first thrust.

Trust that I am young-

but I just might be ready.

Picturing your tongue

up and down my athletic belly.

Taste my rainbow-
lucky charms.
My fire is spreading-
ring the alarm.

A wild fire-
can you put me out?
Relax my mind
with every word from your mouth.

I'll sit on top of you
like a couch.
Put it in me
like a pouch.

Remember, I'm only
words on paper.
Temptation has me feigning.
Temptation is a traitor.

What's my relation

to sweet temptation?

It has my mind cautious

and keeps my body waiting.

That sweet temptation

Heartbroken

A dozen roses for what?

I've just been wasting precious time

for all of these years.

Being judged as foolish just because I thought I had something special.

I thought I was gifted, thought I founded my answers.

Nothing but broken wishes.

I feel like broken dishes.

And now I look back at it

like man I was addicted.

I had given my all

but your love was insufficient.

Why waste my time and make me the target?

When nobody had your back

I rode for you the hardest.

Luckily at the time I wasn't the smartest.

I was too busy painting my relationship like some type of artist.

Heartbroken I was-

I was scorched by your love, but I will move on and sure enough

I will find myself a dove.

Dope Girl

I am the dope girl-

I supply for the fiends.

I will make my profit by all means.

I've been carrying the weight

for nineteen years.

Watched myself as my face shed tears.

Like bacteria, I will grow on you.

I got that snow white

that will snow on you.

I am the dope girl

but I don't mess with drugs.

The best way to get high is by kisses and hugs.

I got that dime bag-

the exclusive edition.

High like a bird, feel the heat in my kitchen.

Inhale my smoke-

I'm obviously on fire.

I weaken your lungs when I speak.

Let my product roll off your tongue.

Do you feel me take over your body?

Naughty? Not me.

Puff Puff, but don't pass me.

Gently focus and grab me-

you can have me.

I am not ecstasy

but I can be your fantasy.

The best dope you will ever meet.

You will feel me

throughout your body.

Every single limb, throbbing.

I am the dope girl-

the real thing.

Guaranteed to fulfill every dream.

I'll watch your eyes get low-

then I'll drop and pull up slow.

My dope is like whoa!

I'm sadly addictive-

but I'm not death threatening.

I am where your mind should be.

My dope won't kill-

well maybe mentally.

Once you puff, you won't get enough of me.

I am the dope girl.

Keep this between me and you-

and come get high with me.

The dope girl

Heartless

You don't care about the time
I've put in to make things work.
You just care about yourself
and deep inside it hurts.

You look at me and see a picture,
but do you recognize the art?
Or do you not pay attention?
You must see right through my heart.

Do my words mean anything?
Because my mind is saying no.
Do you want to hold on?
Because my heart is letting go.

I refuse to take the pain.
I've been rained on too many times.
They told me it would happen
but I just ignored your lies.

How could you hurt someone

who gave their all for you?

But I guess you're like the rest

because you're heartless too.

Without You

Without you I am in danger.

You guard my heart without a doubt.

You put my mind at ease-

forcing me to smile.

At first my heart was at risk-

I'd say my heart was at war.

But you defeated the enemy

and now I don't have to suffer anymore.

You brought light into my darkness

and because of you I dream.

At first I didn't know how to act-

but it's clear, your love is such a beautiful thing.

The sound of your voice has the power to heal.

You make life worth living, you make love so real.

Every breath I take, I take it for you.

If I ever should lose you, what will I do?

My heart is so much bigger
My blood is so much richer
My smile glows brighter
My love is much thicker

Without you life is too lonely-
who wants to live life alone?
Now that I've got you, I plan to keep you.
So help me stay strong.

Without you I can't think-
matter of fact, I can't even sleep.
I think of you twenty-four seven-
every day of the week.

No one can compare to you.
You are simply one of a kind.
You could be someone else's love-
I'm very thankful that your mine.

How could I live if

you weren't by my side?

If you cry, I cry.

If you die, so do I?

You're my other half.

You're the best of me.

So I'd be glad to announce to the world that

without you, there is no me.

Anonymous

When I think of you

I think of heaven.

For you to claim me in your life

is a blessing.

But still I haven't learned thy lesson.

You play games with my mind-

so I'm always guessing.

Do you feel the same way as I do for you?

Am I wasting my time longing for you?

You brighten my day when I hear your voice.

If you were a Hershey's kiss

you'd be my number one choice.

What I see in you, is something so deep.

If you were the wind

you'd sweep me off of my feet.

Sometimes you seem as if
you hold yourself back.
You bury your emotions
but I see through the cracks.

I just want to love you
and be your support.
Let me be your judge
when you go to court.

What I am trying to say is that
I want to be your light in the dark.
The blood that flows to your heart.
You're parking break when you park.

So please don't push me away,
I just want you to stay.
Come spread your wings with me,
and we can both fly away.

You're giving me second thoughts,

so please convince me to stay.

Insecure

Okay, I've tried to hold it in
but I've simply had enough.
If you can't trust in my loyalty-
that's it, you're out of luck.

I'm sick of being the victim
when all I do is play my part.
Your insecurities
are really tearing us apart.

What do you expect me
to do?
Because first off-
if I wanted out,
I'd simply leave you.
No need to beat around the bush
and play those childish games.
You have some self issues-
but that bullshit needs to change.

You get mad at me

just because other guys attempt to speak with me.

I look at them quickly

and admit I am taken.

Do not get me mistaken

for your sorry chicks in the past.

Mistaking me

with the past trends

will get you stuck-

with a foot up your ass!

Am I angry?

Yes I am because I'm tired of it all.

I've been way too true to you

for you to try to play me foul.

I can only take so much-

and you need to realize what you have.

I'm loyal and I'm genuine, there is no pretending.

But if I have to, I won't hesitate

to make you a part of my past.

You and your insecurities

I Want It

I want it like caramel on an apple-

tight like the top on a bottle of Snapple.

I want it like fruit loops-

fruity and good in the mouth.

I want it like popcorn-

be my butter, make me stutter.

Make me hit a high note like a piano-

I'll make you growl like an animal.

I want it like chocolate cake-

maybe ice cream on the side.

Let me step inside-

I'll melt in your mouth.

I want it like fried chicken-

be my hot sauce, I'll knock the top off.

Get it like ribs with barbeque sauce-

a little spice on your tongue.

I want it like a water park-
the electricity to my spark.
The roller coaster to my park-
the golden key to my heart.

I want it like a baby-
soft and very gentle.
Then I want it like basketball-
be aggressive a little.

I want it like kool-aid-
tasty and real sweet.
Then I want it like a calendar-
every day of the week.

I want it like a Nike shoe-
fresh out the box, clean and new.
But I don't want it if you're not my man.
That's just not what ladies do!

Why

Why?

Last time I checked, I thought that was a question.

Yet, you looked at me blankly, simply a rejection.

I don't hate you; no one is made of perfection

but I wish you'd grow up and teach yourself a lesson.

Lady is tired of stressing over your childish mess.

I'm not a game nor a scantron

so why put me to the test?

You act less like a weak actress.

Might as well switch it up, I wear the pants and you the dress.

Now let me do what I please-

I don't care, boy you can leave.

So I can leave? Boy please, this is not new to me.

You think my love is for granted?

I'll take it from you like you never had it.

I warned you to grab it, but all you did was stab it.

You probably don't realize it-

but I'm telling you now.

I will move on to the next

show you how I get down.

No point in sticking around.

Walking around with a frown, this is my time now.

You'll realize when I'm gone

that you needed me home.

Cause now you're lost and lonely,

wishing you could just hold me.

So while you got what you got-

you better pay attention.

No time for little boys-

my heart is on a mission.

So if I have to I'll put you in submission,

and lock you out cold, punish you

DETENTION!

Pressure

Sitting here on my empty bed-

so many thoughts surround my head.

Surround sound in my mind-

I can't even turn it down.

So I look directly in the mirror

and looking back is a clown.

Yes I'll say it-

I'm a virgin.

But it's hard in these streets

because all these guys want to do is freak.

They thirsty to divide the legs-

but never ready to support a possible baby.

Always asking me this

and telling me that.

But I don't feel you like that

and I'm not ready for that.

Plus I'm saving it for marriage

and if you think that is too long-

then carry your sorry ass

back to the last girl you boned.

I said

stop trying to pressure me.

Just because I'm fresh meat

doesn't mean that

you have an advantage.

And just because you pressure me-

it doesn't mean that I will panic.

I will manage because

good things come to those who wait.

And if you hate me for holding out-

then bye, get out of my face.

I am not doing this for

you.

I am holding out for

me.

I'm being careful-

the last thing I want is HIV.

You may be blind,

but I can see-

and so can he.

One day a MAN will come along

and see me for ME.

And he will get on bended knee

and set my virginity free.

Blind

Here we go again, another argument!

I really don't want to hear it, so I pop my music in my ear.

Well maybe my music is why I still remain unclear.

I'm listening to her, but at the same time I'm not-

Deep inside, all I want is for this argument to stop.

I told her I don't know how to put myself into words-

well maybe I should look from her view, but I don't have the nerves.

I know that she cares for me, but somehow I'm still losing-

like I want to take loves road, but my mind is cruising.

What am I doing?

One of the best things that has ever happened to me.

Last time I let her fly away-

I was hoping that I'd get lucky

and that she'd come back my way.

Luckily!

Now I have her, but I feel like I'm not ready.

And it's cutting me deeply, breaking me like candy.

In a way I'm afraid to lose her-

for the fact that I know, guys are waiting in line to choose her.

Abuse her, love her!

But she was honest; she told me she only wanted me.

Told me I was the one that could fulfill her every need-

I find that hard to see

because of what I've been through.

I'm sorry love, but I don't mean to hurt you.

I tell her this over and over-

I know she's sick of it, I hope she won't say it's over.

All I really want to do

is hug her and bring her closer

but times get heated, and I'm toasted like a toaster.

We had our good times, and still we had our bad.

What I must understand is what I have.

I'm not trying to let this go, but it is killing me slow-

she keeps telling me, there is no love if it doesn't show.

We talked about our future, but I think it's in danger-

sometimes I feel like I'm lost, like I'm just her stranger.

So she shakes her head slowly-

inside she burns with anger.

What can I do to please you?

I don't understand, but I need you!

The other dudes don't know how to treat you.

But who am I to speak because I can't even keep you.

Love & Loyalty

Though I have seen so many heart breaks

and dated so many childish minds-

I still have faith in love.

Their ignorance won't make me blind.

For I know that every guy is different

but the chance of finding a real one-

is a very low percentage.

I won't give up, love doesn't come easy

because I work for love.

And whenever he shall find me

I'll be his number one employee.

Call me love and loyalty!

For if I breathe about you

I am your oxygen.

If you can't sleep without me

I am your thoughts.

And I shall trust him with my heart-my masterpiece, his work of art.

I will taste him on my tongue every time I take

a bite out of each day.

He will be my army

that helps me fight through each day.

I'll be every answer

to his quiz or survey.

Portray no false image-

that is the devil's spinach.

The world is dying quickly

and I must keep love in it.

I am the dying breed-

there is not many like me.

If you look past my appearance

you'll see deep inside me.

Deep enough to catch each tear that I have ever cried.

Every time I gave up

just to make up.

Not meaning that I quit,

but just to save us.

When I say us-

I mean me and myself.

Didn't want to be a heartbreak-

so I saved myself.

I left.

Now I'm patiently waiting for that

love and affection.

Pain is a lesson

to lean towards protection.

If I'm your obsession

come and join my session.

And we can become one

and teach the world a lesson.

The Greatest Man

I must say

I have never been so happy with a man.

Not only is he that,

but also my best friend.

He has never doubted me

and never has he been insecure.

Every time a door closes-

he opens a new door.

He has taught me so much-

and I must say I'm very thankful.

A love so strong-

being blessed all along.

He brought me into his home-

and showed me his favorite book.

He has helped me through hard times-

and without him I would perish.

He is the greatest man alive.

His name is God-

the one I cherish.

THE

END

"Even the longest roads must end somewhere."

Nneka J. Howell (Lady Poet) was born on May 17, 1990 on the south side of Chicago, IL. Nneka is currently a sophomore at the University of Illinois in Champaign-Urbana, IL. She plans to continue to use her writing as a stepping stone for others. When it comes to what she writes, her number one mission is to reach others so that someone else may be inspired by her creative works. She believes that poetry is more than just words, but a blessing in disguise that many tend to push aside. To her, poetry is a key to one's heart, and the directions to inspiration.

Liberated Publishing Inc
1860 Wilma Rudolph Blvd
Clarksville, TN 37040
info@liberatedpublishing.com
931-378-0500

www.LiberatedPublishing.com

www.ingramcontent.com/pod-product-compliance
Lightning Source LLC
LaVergne TN
LVHW051549070426
835507LV00021B/2494